A V... The Face Of Life

A Spiritual & Reflective Journey

by

Hazel F. Adams

Dell R. Adams

To: VERONICA

I hope you are inspired
when reading this book.

Keep the Faith
   Dell Ray
 " 4/15/2019 "

A Walk In
The Face of Life

By

Hazel F. Adams

&

Dell R. Adams

Published By

Adams Publishing

Nashville, Tennessee

Forward

This collection of poems, writings, sayings and thoughts are the works of Hazel F. Adams and Dell R. Adams.

After many years of writing and responding to events that occurred in our lives, we decided to share these ideas with you. Many of the friends and family that we write about are just like people you know, have known or will know during your life time.

Our purpose is to capture moments in history and offer hope, love, share ideas, life experiences and provide a source of thought, reflection, and inspiration to others.

ISBN#: 978-0-615-92271-3

For permission, email:

Dell R. Adams: dadams3487@comcast.net

German Adams: adamsmarketing123@comcast.net

ACKNOWLEDGEMENTS

To family, friends, acquaintances and all the wonderful people we have had the pleasure of knowing, spending time with, crying with, and praying with, we owe you so much. Life is a beautiful journey, and we continue to acknowledge each of you in the spirit of love and hope.

Editing

Cheryl L. Adams & Erica A. Adams

Typesetting

Erica A. Adams

Bible Verse Selections

Larry A. Adams & Erica A. Adams

Illustrations

Evan E. Adams

Photo Cover & Design

German Adams

CONTENTS

DEDICATION

A Walk In The Face Of Life, A Spiritual and Reflective Journey is dedicated to the life and memory of Hazel F. Adams. A devoted mother, nurse and church member, she was a drum major for humanity and justice throughout her life. Her life exemplified excellence and family values. In December 2005, Hazel F. Adams was elevated to a higher power. However, her spirit, compassion and love for others remains with us forever.

Chapter I

In Memory of Someone

In memory of those who have gone on before us, friends, family and loved ones that we hold near and dear to our hearts forever. Whose thoughts, deeds and memory we will long remember.

This chapter is in memory of Captain Marcus Ray Alford, US Army, who served his family and country with honor.
(1982-2010)

"The memory of the just is blessed, but the name of the wicked shall rot."

-Proverbs 10:7

In Honor Of Those Who Lived And Died
In America
September 11, 2001

By Dell R. Adams

Oh God of all Faiths, we pray this day for your wisdom, mercy, and divine grace. The attack on the World Trade Center and the Pentagon was a tragedy that shocked America, the World, and the entire Human Race.

During this time of fear, anger, love, hate, and disbelief, we must all pull together with hope and faith in spite of our grief on this day. It's time for healing and blessings for the special people who gave their life and time to those in harm's way.

To the firemen, policemen, doctors, nurses, construction workers, servicemen, women and all who dared to care; we salute you with honor, love, and holy prayer. Yours was a noble cause carried out for those who suffered and died in a time of great despair.

What manner of hate, envy, and jealousy can bring anyone to the point of killing and depriving thousands of people of all faiths, cultures, and ethnicities to their end without a chance in life?

We don't know the reason for this awful day in history, but we do know that America and the World will never be the same. So we pray for the innocent people whose lives were shattered in a moment of hatred and evil by the weak and the wicked of the world. On this unimaginable day we ask for Peace and Love in thy holy name.

Now we must pick up the pieces, move on with our lives

and focus without fear, hate, anger, mistrust and sorrow. This task will be a challenging one, which will require a spiritual commitment based on trust and faith in God to grant us a better tomorrow.

The answer is waiting and the call for a new beginning is clearly within our grasp. We must keep the faith, continue to believe in the goodness that dwells within our mist, and honor our call to duty. Our dignity and respect for humanity and God will linger and forever last.

For those who committed these heinous, cowardly, inhumane acts against this Nation and the World, we pray for forgiveness and a new spirit throughout. We know in the end that justice will prevail; there is no doubt.

As we rebuild and begin anew, the memory of this tragic day will never go away. Never have we seen people come together in the entire World with strength, courage, and conviction to stand up against the evil committed on this day. Our response to this terrible event in the coming days, months, and years is a true test of our faith and ability to weather the storm in the midst of great strife.

In this time of great uncertainty, let us come back to where we began. Say a prayer, hug a friend, say hello to a neighbor and never forget how we got here and where we came from.

Peace, Love, Mercy, and Grace to the many victims and families who suffered on this horrendous day. We pray always for the many brave men, women, and children who sacrificed their lives so that we may be free. May this tragedy teach America and the World that violence, hatred, and disrespect for humanity is not the answer. There must be a better way.

A Tribute To Bob

by

Dell R. Adams

I remember Bob as a cousin, a friend, and a brother, but he was much more than that, Bob was an inspiration to all who knew him and his memory will never pass away.

Bob loved his family, his church, his friends, his community, as he loved life each and every day. He was always reaching out and giving to others without regard for self. He gave and gave and gave even when there was nothing left.

Bob was a man of few words, soft-spoken, but you always knew how he felt. Sometimes the smile did the trick, or perhaps it was the silence that let you know. Bob was a man of deeds and action who lived by example and learned spiritually to grow and grow.

I remember Bob as a man with strong moral character -a person with integrity, dignity and pride. Bob was a shinning light that always shined bright. If ever in trouble or need, he was the guy you wanted on your side. If you ever needed a friend or brother, or just someone to talk to, Bob was the man for the job. The next time you see that shining light on a hill, don't worry its probably "Bob."

"What shall we then say to these things? If God be for us, who can be against us?"

-Romans 8: 31

A Tribute To "Wixie"

by

Dell R. Adams

If you listen carefully you can hear her calling to breakfast, to supper, to wash before bed. If you slightly remember, you can see her toiling, washing, sewing, ironing, churning milk to butter, flour to bread.

For someone who gave so much, she wanted so little in return. A warm smile, a thank you, a nod or just some concern. Each day of her life was filled with caring. For her true rewards in life were giving and sharing.

Though she bore no children by birth, she was mother, counselor, doctor and friend to many on earth. Though she won no awards or Nobel prizes, her values and positive impact on others were the true measures of her worth.

With her strong firm hand, she was always in command. Whether you called her Wixie or Wick you knew she was strict, but more importantly you knew she was right. Yes, she was strict but also quick — to aid and defend you.

Although she is no longer with us physically, she is still working and toiling. If you listen carefully even now you can hear her calling.

"He that followeth after righteousness and mercy findeth life, righteousness and honor."

-Proverbs 21:21

To My Grandmother
by
Dell R. Adams

You are a very special grandmother who has brought so much joy to my heart and peace to my mind. Always there when needed, always there when my ways seem blind. You open my pathway to greatness with love so kind.

I remember your many words of wisdom, and your strong belief in God. Always giving guidance, with a wink, a nod, a hint, or just a word. No matter how one reacted to your teachings, you always knew that you were heard.

Of the words and phrases I often heard you say, none clings to my mind and memory as this one "Tell The Truth And Stay In The Church." This message I think of daily and it means so very much.

I have shared in your triumphs, your successes and your tears. I salute you on this day and may God forever bless you in His own special way.

"Exalt her, and she shall promote thee: she shall bring thee to honor, when thou dost embrace her."

-Proverbs 4:8

Big Momma
by
Dell R. Adams

She was never formally educated by Yale, Harvard or any Ivy league school. Her degree was earned by mastering the art of loving and caring, that was her rule. From the most of us to the very least of us, the goal was justice and truth.

Throughout her life she lived by example, stamping her goodness label on all who passed her way. She was a strong and courageous woman who feared God and cherished life day by day.

Cooking , cleaning, washing, scrubbing, sewing and building a firm foundation. Always encouraging others to reach for a good education. She was a true diplomat, building on her strengths and always developing good relations.

We all loved her because of her character and commitment to justice and truth. She was a simple, but complex woman, who was respectfully known as Ruth.

" Even by the God of thy father, who shall keep thee; and by
the Almighty, who shall bless thee with blessings of heaven
above, blessings of the deep that lieth under, blessings of the
breasts, and of the womb."

-Genesis 49:5

Chapter II

Blessings From Above

Blessings from God who gives us life, love and all we know in the spirit of reflection through prayer, hope, mercy and promise for the future.

"For by grace are ye saved through faith, and that not of yourself; it is the gift of God."

-Ephesians 2: 8

God's Grace
by

Hazel F. Adams

God, as I travel life's journey I need more of your loving grace. You said your grace is sufficient to run this Christian race. Your grace gives me the strength and courage to do thy will. In spite of the pain, suffering, and agony, I am trusting in you still.

Through your grace and mercy, blessings continue to flow. Your grace is with me on this journey and that's all I need to know. Your grace is with me in the morning, noon, and throughout the night.

As this Christian journey gets harder, I need your grace to finish this race. When the way gets dark and it seems I can't find my way, I need your grace. God with your grace I can do all things, I can finish, I can win this race. This journey is victorious because of your grace.

"For His anger endureth but a moment; in His favor is life: weeping may endure for a night, but joy cometh in the morning."

-Psalms 30:5

Joy

by

Hazel F. Adams

I read in the Holy scriptures how God brought His children through - working miracles, bringing love, peace and Joy to me and you. When our load gets heavy and stumbling blocks seem to fall, his Joy gives us hope and clears a path along our way.

His Joy comes in the morning, noon, evening, and into the night. Joy touches all who believe in Him and are willing to do His will. There is Joy all about us, just keep Him in your sight. In the midst of heartaches and disappointments is Joy is waiting, still.

Rejoice and be glad in him for his Joy shall set you free. Praise God for his goodness and glorify him with Joy for all to see. God's Joy is abundant and spreads throughout the world. God loves all his children, and brings Joy to you and me.

"For we hear that there are some which walk among you disorderly, working not at all, but are busybodies."

-II Thessalonians 3:11

Too Busy

by

Hazel F. Adams

I was just too busy, I didn't take time to pray. I just went on about my business doing the things I do day after day after day. Too busy in the things of the world to listen to what the Lord had to say.

I didn't take time for Jesus, who died to set me free, I was too busy to think about Calvary. Then one day I met the Savior who took my sins away. He washed me clean and started me on the right way.

Now I take time to pray and thank Jesus, for He turned my life around. I am never too busy to serve Him and I pray for His love daily. Now I am too busy serving Him because His mercy and grace keeps me safe and sound.

"Praying always with all prayer and supplication in the Spirit, and watching thereunto with all perseverance and supplication for all saints...."

- Ephesians 6:18

Press On

by

Hazel F. Adams

Press On when trials and tribulations get in your way. Press On in the name of Jesus with the hope of a brighter day.

When this way gets dark and dreary and you can't see the light of day, Press On. Press On for there is light at the end of the tunnel, and God will always make a way.

Press On for he can make rough roads smooth and crooked ways straight. He can make mountains into valleys and valleys into mountains. If you just have patience and the will to wait. Press On.

As you Press On, don't get weary- Press On and don't ever stop, Press On in spite of failures for he will see you to the mountain top. Press On.

Don't ever give up, just Press On boldly and keep heaven in your view. Don't ever doubt him, just Press On, and God will see you through.

Press On.

" What shall we then say to these things? If God be for us who can be against us?"

-Romans 8:31

To Blessed To Be Stressed

by

Hazel F. Adams

I am too blessed to be stressed. There is so much joy in the air and your peace is always there. I thank God for his goodness and mercy that flows from everywhere.

He always blesses me in the morning, through the day, and watches over me at night. And in the mist of my storms, he makes everything alright.

I don't worry about worldly stress or trials of the day. I thank God for his many blessings and the stress just goes away.

Oh sometimes I get weary and burdened along the way, but I refuse to be stressed. For when I see the beauty of this earth, I know that I am eternally blessed.

"Happy is the man that findeth wisdom, and the man that getteth understanding."

-Proverbs 3:13

Prayer For Happiness

by

Hazel F. Adams

Lord help me to live happy each and every day.
Teach me your holy word and your will to obey.
Let happiness abide in our lives eternally.

As we help others throughout each day, Lord help
us to think of them as we kneel and pray. When we
pray Lord, let us bring happiness to others in a kind
and thoughtful way.

When we pray for happiness in the lives of those we
care for and love, may it brighten up their day with
your grace from above. Dear Lord as we pray for
happiness that only you can give, may it touch some
lonely soul each day we live.

"And this I pray, that your love may abound yet more and more in knowledge and in all judgment."

-Philippians 1:9

Prayer For Love

by

Hazel F. Adams

Dear Lord shower us with your precious love.
Please guide us day by day, keep us Lord in all
things your Holy will to always obey. Please fill
our hearts with your love .

Let us not forget your will, may our hearts overflow
with your love. Lord make us calm and still as we
pray for your love from above.

Lord we pray that your love will deliver us from
senseless hate, death and destruction throughout
the world. Through prayer your love can bring
peace to every man, woman, boy and girl.

We need your love to guide us to the path of
righteousness. A path of love for all humanity to
witness and see. Lord we need thee, this is our
prayer for love.

"And Jesus said unto them, 'Come ye after me, and I will make you to become fishers of men .' And straightway they forsook their nets and followed Him."

- Mark 1:17-18

Follow Me
by

Hazel F. Adams

Jesus said "follow me" and I will lead the way.
Follow me and don't get weary, I'll go with you
every day. Follow me and I will guide you, I'll stay
close by your side. Follow me through tribulations,
and in my love abide.

Have no fear for my grace is sufficient, my grace will
protect you on your way. God's amazing grace and
mercy will be with you day by day.

When you follow me, the way may not always be
easy. There will be hardships, yes, and struggles too.
But he promised to be with you, just have faith
because his word is true.

Follow me for I am a way maker, I will lead you
safely through grief and pain. I will direct and guide
you safely through the storms and the rain.

When the journey is complete and the victory of life
you have won, remember when you follow Jesus
greater works can be done.

Follow me through pain and sorrow, and true
victory you can claim. And when the journey is over
praise and magnify his Holy name.

And when the path gets rocky and rough, don't
stumble, don't fall, look to the cross of Calvary
where Jesus died to save us all.

"I will lift up mine eyes unto the hills, from whence cometh my help. My help cometh from the Lord, which made heaven and earth."

-Psalm 121: 1-2

Life's Journey
by

Hazel F. Adams

As you travel on life's journey keep heaven in your view. And the good you do for others will be measured back to you. Help a friend, a neighbor or someone you don't even know and God will bless you through and through.

Yes life's journey may get tedious, but remember God will help you on your way. As you seek his love and mercy, he will guide you every day. On the journey He will keep you on the straight and narrow, and never let you go astray.

Oh you must keep on toiling, but just keep love in all you do. You may get tired along the way but if you believe in God you will never get tired of the way. Life's journey can be a comforting adventure if you put God in front of you.

"Pray without ceasing. In everything give thanks; for this is the will of God in Christ Jesus concerning you."

I Thessalonians 5: 17-18

"Jubilee Prayer"

by

Hazel F. Adams

Dear Master as we approach a new beginning and a new day is dawning, let us spring clean our lives and correct our mistakes. Let us look unto you for we know that your grace is sufficient to keep us in the future as it has kept us in the past. Help us in this Jubilee Year celebration to keep our minds stayed on Thee. Giving you the praise, the honor and the glory for we realize that only you made this year of Jubilee possible. We thank Thee, Father for the bright days and we thank the for the dark days, for we know that the dark days have made our bright days even brighter along the way. We thank Thee, O God, for being ever near us, hovering over us and protecting us in the mist of our storms. You are always with us and we know that underneath us are your ever lasting arms. Dear Lord, make each of us the Christians you would have us to be. Give us that love that sustain in a dying hour. Please let this new beginning and this new year bring us closer to each other and closer to Thee. In your name we trust. This is my prayer in Jesus' name. Amen.

"He maketh peace in thy borders, and filleth thee with the finest of the wheat."

Psalms 147:14

God Gives Inner Peace

by

Hazel F. Adams

When the storms of life surround you and you are filled with needless fear, just look to God your heavenly father for he is always near.

He gives peace that is unlimited, He gives you courage day by day, He will calm the storms around you If to him you humbly pray. He will provide that inner peace that drives the storm away in the quietness of the hour, let Jesus have his way.

Just think how he created you in his image and likeness too, and just have faith and trust in Him and he will provide inner peace for you. He gives peace that bridges all understanding, He will never leave you alone, He gives peace to all who love him, and he never forgets his own.

Just pray for strength and guidance and his loving arms will reach out in every way. Just give him the praise and he will grant you inner peace and protection day by day.

"But seek ye first the Kingdom of God, and his righteousness; and all these things shall be added unto you."

-Matthew 6: 33

Patience

by

Hazel F. Adams

Be patient with me-God is not through with me yet, he has a great work for me to do and His grace will see me through.

Although I may suffer what seems like endless pain, he said press on— "your work will not be in vain." Oh his grace is sufficient for me, because he paid the price on Calvary.

He bore such suffering and ridicule... he suffered so much shame. He died that we all might live, be healed and be made whole again.

So trust God to give you patience and please be patient with me. For with God's grace and mercy we will gain true victory!

"Thou wilt keep him in perfect peace, whose mind is stayed on thee: because he trusteth in thee."

-Isaiah 26:3

Chapter III

Peace and Strength

As we reach and search to find peace and strength in our lives, we often look beyond the here and now. In many instances, it leads us back to where we began.

"I can do all things through Christ which strengthen me."
- Philippians 4: 13

Calm Of The Day
by
Dell R. Adams

When in distress I need a spirit to calm my nerves and grant me rest. Often times it's all I can do to reach my true potential and search for an answer to relieve my stress.

The true love of God and the Holy blessings that always come our way is the only thing that touches us and relieves the pressures of the day.

So reach and search and you will surely see that only he can calm your nerve and create a blessing that will always pass your way.

If you want true peace and calm from all that seems so hard, know within your heart that all blessings truly come from God.

"Fear not; for thou shalt not be ashamed: neither be thou confounded; for thou shalt not be put to shame: for thou shalt forget the shame of thou youth, and shalt not remember the reproach of thy widowhood anymore."

-Isaiah 54:4

Shame

by

Dell R. Adams

Put down your shame, no cause to blame. Lift up your spirit and treat all people the same. Don't be afraid of who you are, but lift up your voice and be heard here and afar.

What is your claim? Are you seeking fortune, glory or fame? Are you truly happy with who you are, or are you faking life simply to be treated the same?

Look deeply within your soul, search and find the true meaning of your life. Don't get caught up in the shame blame game.

For who we are is not the thing, but what you can be is the true measure of your worth. Lift up your spirit, rejoice, be glad and sing. No shame.

"Be not forgetful to entertain strangers: for thereby some have entertained angels unaware."

Hebrews 13: 2

The Shadow Knows
by
Dell R. Adams

Life is but a walking shadow, that reflects on our
way of living day by day. How we treat ourselves
and others lightens or darkens our path along the
way.

So open up your heart, soul and mind. Give thanks
for who you are and always be loving and kind.
Look back on your life and search, step forward,
live for truth be courageous and bold.

Live for today, but plan for tomorrow. Reach for the
stars and forget about the sorrow. If you sow the
good seed, the shadow will fill your trail with silver
and gold.

Life is but a walking shadow, so be the best in all
you do. For how you treat others is a true reflection
on you.

The Shadow Knows.

"A new commandment I give unto you, That ye love one another; as I have loved you, that ye also love one another."

-John 13:34

Show Some Love
by
Dell R. Adams

When all seems dark and you can't see the light, show love, trust in God and he will make things right. By showing love, we can reconcile our differences and reach a higher plain. For by giving and showing love, we can enjoy the sunshine and truly appreciate the rain.

Love generates that healing power that brings us closer together, minute by minute and hour by hour. Love's light shines through and stands tall on our holy tower.

Show some love for all the world is caught up in fear and doubt. Show your love, for that's what we all should be about.

"Wisdom is with aged men, with long life is understanding."

Job 12:12

Never Grow Old
by

Dell R. Adams

Never grow old, be truthful to yourself, live life to the fullest be strong courageous and bold. Live life as though your dreams are forever and your world will never seem cold. Don't ever accept defeat, for giving in shall only make you weaker and you can't ever be that person in your soul.

The power of the mind is the strongest force known to woman and man. The power of your will is immeasurable and can never be taken away. Live as though your past was not history, but only a mirror of yesterday.

Keep the future in your sight, believe with all you have and all your might. Sit for a while, dare to dream, for in your heart you know it's right. Keep your mind sharp, play with a child, renew your spirit and show that wonderful smile.

Believe in yourself, never doubt keep your eye on the prize rise up from your shame and disbelief. Don't trust in what you hear, don't be swayed by what you are told. Have faith in yourself and you will never grow old.

"Behold, I will bring it health and cure, and I will cure them, and will reveal unto them the abundance of peace and truth."

-Jeremiah 33:6

Am I Perfect
by

Dell R. Adams

Am I perfect ? You bet I am not and neither are you.
Do I have character flaws? You know I do, and you
have them too. Is perfection determined by what I
am worth, or is it based on what I do.

Often I don't measure up to the standards that have
been set. Many times I miss the mark and fail to
reach that shining star. But I have no regrets, for
it's not a reflection on my perfection but on my
aim to sometimes reach too far.

Perfection by anyone is seldom achieved, it can
be learned but it's very hard to teach. Don't be
distressed if your aim doesn't met your reach.
Keep striving for perfection, don't give in, its not
the ultimate goal but it's often preached.

For none of us will ever reach true perfection, it just
wasn't meant to be that way. Too many of us it's a
dream to work towards each and every day. Is
perfection doing it right at the right time all the
time? Or is it just giving your best with all you have
in every way.

Am I perfect? I don't think so. Will I ever be perfect?
I don't think so. But I am striving to reach that
plateau. Am I perfect? No but neither are you.

"For God hath not given us the spirit of fear; but of power, and of love, and of a sound mind."

II Timothy 1: 7

Danger Zone
by

Dell R. Adams

When faced with clear and present danger, put down your fears, press forward and bury your tears. Plant your faith in Jesus and he will convert your grief and sorrow to blessings and cheers. If you trust in Him, He promised to make your enemies bow at your feet. He will never leave you and you won't have to retreat.

The danger zone is not the end, but a new beginning that gives us a sign of our courage and ability to cope with adversity. So when in that zone, don't try to go it alone. Keep the faith in Him for He is always on the throne.

A mighty fortress is our God, for He watches us like the sparrow, and keeps us in the straight and narrow. Don't ever fear the danger zone for He will grant you mercy and you will never walk alone.

"Humble yourselves therefore under the mighty hand of God, that he may exalt you in due time. Casting all your cares upon him; for he cares for you. Be sober, be vigilant; because your adversary the devil, as a roaring lion, walketh about, seeking whom he may devour."

-I Peter 5: 6-8

Violence Watch
by

Dell R. Adams

I watch and I see, I listen and I hear. I wonder and I ponder. What can this be? What value do we place on life? Such a precious gift to be treasured and measured-but ended so quickly by a gun or a knife.

Where do we draw the line in the sand? Where do we stop and see and listen to the reality that life is true and wholesome and grand? None of us, you or me is perfect, but we all have the right to be all that we can be.

Who has the right to take away the chance so early before we can truly listen and see what life has to offer the young, the talented, the gifted, and the free.

Who knows what each and everyone can achieve if given a chance to reach beyond our here and near. We all need that chance to go beyond and reach out to listen and hear.

Stop the violence now. Listen to your heart and watch the beauty of life command your soul somehow. Watch the violence and see and hear what it's doing to you and me.

"Honor all men. Love the brotherhood. Fear God. Honor the King."

-I Peter 2:17

My Brother
by

Dell R. Adams

You are a true friend; in fact you are like a Brother.
I mourn with you today in the loss of your Mother.
You know the Bible says that God is a Spirit.
We should praise and worship Him like no other.
If you truly believe that, and I know that you do,
He will provide you with strength and comfort too.
There are no rivers or oceans too wide to cross.
And there are no burdens too much to bare.
Look around and you know He is always there.
Whether it's the wind, sun, rain or the smile of a
Child, God's goodness is with us, even when we rest
a while..
Keep the Faith and remember you are my Brother.

"The wolf also shall dwell with the lamb, and the leopard shall lie down with the kid; and the calf and the young lion and the fatling together; and a little child shall lead them."

-Isaiah 11:6

Chapter IV

A Child Shall Lead Them

It's all about the children. They are the present and the future. Without them we have no one to lead us, for through their eyes we can see forever.

" When I was a child, I spake as a child, I thought as a child: but when I became a man, I put away childish things."

-I Corinthians 13:11

It Took A While
by

Dell R. Adams

It took a while, but man was once a child.

From crib to cradle, crawling, walking, sooner or later, it took a while.

Tears, fears, cries, laughter, and then a smile, it took a while, but man was once a child.

A seed planted will soon expand, and grow if given a proper hand, and like a child it takes a while.

It takes a while to know, to glow and to find your way.

The bumps, bruises, scars, pain, and falls give us reasons to doubt and fret, but through it all it takes a while, because it's still a child.

A child needs nourishment and comforting each and every day.

What started out long, long ago as a child is now willing and ready to grow and prosper into manhood, ready to take on the world and all it has to offer.

From pain to tears, from doubt to fears, now we can smile.

It took a while but man was once a child.

"If thou faint in the day of adversity, thy strength is small."

Proverbs 24:10

" I Am A Lot Like You"
by

Hazel F. Adams

I have Down's Syndrome, I am slow at learning.
That is true, I have abnormal features but I am really
a lot like you.
I am slow at learning to walk and talk, and cannot
dress as fast as you; but given time and patience I
can learn to tie my shoe. Just take a look at yourself
and perhaps you will see that maybe you didn't
learn at age four what your brother or sister did at
age three.
They tell me there was a chromosome error that
occurs once in every 600 births. So as you see,
there are many like me on this beautiful earth. But
we are not all alike, for we have different limitations
in the things we say and do. We are each unique
individuals, and we are really a lot like you.
We learn, we care, so please forget the myths, the
shock and the agony. Give me the support I need to
cope with my disability. I need growth and
stimulation to feel worthy is my plea.
So touch me, hold me and find a job that I can do.
For with all of my limitations, I am really a lot like
you.
There is no medicine or treatment that can cure my
condition you see, but I can do my best in special
education programs that you design for me.
Please help me to develop skills in the things I am
able to do. Let us start with the simple tasks, for I am
a lot like you.

"Train up a child in the way he should go: and when he is old, he will not depart from it."

-Proverbs 22:6

The Extra Mile Can Help A Child
by

Hazel F. Adams

I am I willing to go the extra mile, if my going can help some child. Help a child to know that someone cares. How the child develops and grows through the early years…

A child needs care, nurturing and all the happiness love can bring. Someone by a child's side to stay. Some one to give guidance along the way.

A child needs support and praise, we must show the child that we care and when the child is in need be ready and awaiting there.

The extra mile may be a great big hug or just a smile. It may be just a word of praise, that can make a child's life worth while.

So you see the extra mile is not a long, long way, but oh, how it can brighten a child's day. So I am willing to go the extra mile, and bring joy and happiness to some little child.

"And verily I say unto you, except ye be converted, and become as little children, ye shall not enter into the kingdom of heaven."

- Matthew 18:3

A Little Child's Prayer At Christmas Time
by
Hazel F. Adams

As I sat playing with my toys,
I thought about other girls and boys.

Some have toys and others don't—
and some know there is no need to want.

No need to want, for wanting is just a dream—
because their parents have no means,

No means for providing toys for them;
No dolls for her, no trucks for him.

But when I say my prayers tonight,
I'll ask God to make it right.

For I have many, many toys, I even have enough
to spare.

"Dear God," make all girls and boys at Christmas
time have toys.

This is my prayer.

"But Jesus said, 'Suffer little children, and forbid them not, to come unto me: for of such is the kingdom of heaven'."

-Matthew 19:14

A Child's Eyes
by

Hazel F. Adams

In the eyes of a child, we see a world full of hope
and love. Through their eyes, the possibilities are
unlimited and the opportunities are boundless.

In a child's eyes the sun shines bright by day and
when its night the stars twinkle and the moon is full
of light. In the eyes of a child, if we look beyond
the clouds, we can see a sparrow, a robin or a dove.

Within their eyes there is no hate, jealousy or envy,
we see a world filled with peace and love. Through
their eyes, we don't feel the pressures of the day, for
in their eyes God is always taking care of us from
above.

See the world with the eyes of a child and
remove the fear and doubt that makes us weak.
Through the eyes of a child, we can all live in peace
and share the beauty that God grants each of us —
the strong, the humble and the meek.

"Love suffers long and is kind; love does not envy; love does not parade itself, is not puffed up... bear all things, believes all things, hopes all things, endures all things.
Love never fails..."

-I Corinthians 13: 4, 7-8

Chapter V

Love Someone

To love someone is truly special. It's a bond that heals the soul. In many ways it is the force that guides our values and makes life worth living. Giving love is the ultimate gift and it's extra special when it comes from the heart. Without love, there is no truth and in its absence, we can never be truly free.

"As the lily amongst thorns, so is my love amongst the daughters."

- Song of Solomon 2:2

To The One I Love

by

Dell R. Adams

Since I met you my life has been more complete. Your lovely smile, your warm gentle touch and the way you look at me means so much. It's like a whole new world has opened up with new possibilities and such.

In all my dreams, I never thought I would care for someone as much as I do you. You are special to me in your own loving way and I think of you each and every day.

It's as though things are upside down, spinning constantly when you are not around. Always wanting to be near you, to hear your voice and lovely sound.

I know it seems like we are not together enough and we spend too much time apart... But you are always with me and close to my heart.

My love for you is everlasting and it will never fade away. Without your love I would be completely lost, not knowing where to begin or start. I love you dearly and my love for you grows stronger each passing day.

To the one I love.

"Set me as a seal upon thine heart, as a seal upon thine arm: for love is strong as death, jealousy is cruel as the grave: the coals thereof are coals of fire, which hath a most vehement flame. Many waters cannot quench love, neither can the floods drown it..."

- Song of Solomon 8: 6-7

My Love To You
by
Dell R. Adams

My love for you is like nothing I have ever known. Since I met you my feelings towards you have just grown and grown. When I am away from you, I long for your gentle touch. It's like nothing in this world I have ever known.

I think of you both day and night. I think of you wrong or right. For thinking of you makes the day and the future bright. As the sun rises and on till night, I think of you and my heart feels it's right.

For it is my desire to share your every dream, and give you all the love that you will ever need. As time and space come closer together my love for you grows deeper and stronger, and I know it will last for ever and even longer.

Love to you ... to you my love.

"Let us get up early to the vineyards; let us see if the vine flourish, whether the tender grape appear, and the pomegranates bud forth: there will I give thee my loves."

-Song of Solomon 7:12

Someone Special

by

Dell R. Adams

To someone so kind, I am proud to call you mine.
For someone who has much, you have given so
much more, of your time, love, care and goodwill
each day.

Your treasure is not filled with silver and gold, but
with strength, courage, faith and respect for the peo-
ple you have touched along the way.

Time to listen to all my fears, troubles and concerns.
Love to fill my voids and calm my worried mind.
Caring is your special gift, and I thank you for al-
ways being so kind.

You are a special person and will always have a
place in my heart.. I've known this a long time, since
the very beginning, from the start. Forever keep that
warm, wonderful smile and continue being the spe-
cial person you are. And we will always be a part of
each other, whether near or far.

" How fair and how pleasant art thou, O love, for delights!"
-Song of Solomon 7:6

Missing You

by

Dell R. Adams

My visions of you are warm, wonderful, and true.
It is truly a joy to know and spend time with you.

You are an inspiration beyond my wildest belief.
When you are away from me I am in constant grief.

As I look and appreciate this beautiful snowy day,
You are on my mind in the most unbelievable way.

How much I want to see you is beyond my scope.
Like you, I keep the faith and maintain much hope.

Until we see each other and rekindle the flame.
I will be missing you and life will never be the same.

"Missing You"

"And the Lord make you to increase and abound in love one toward another, and toward all men, even as we do toward you."

-I Thessalonians 3:12

Love Someone
by
Dell R. Adams

Love someone and watch your world come alive and grow in every way. Without love we live in a world of constant fear and darkness. It's only with love that we can see our way and know the difference from night and day.

When you love someone you open up the floodgates of joy and promises unknown. With love you enter into a new beginning full of treasures beyond measure. Love opens doors and gives a new sense of focus and direction in our pathway.

Give love and love will come back to you in more ways than you will ever know. Love is what love gives. Try loving someone and see your world grow and grow.

"One who is righteous is a guide to his neighbor, but the way of the wicked leads them astray."

-Proverbs 12:26

Chapter VI

Friends, Neighbors and Others

Friends, neighbors and others that come in our path are some how tied to our destiny. How we treat them in good times and bad shapes our lives in many ways. If we show them love, respect and admiration, our future will follow that pattern.

"But Jesus beheld them, and said unto them, with men this is impossible; but with God all things are possible."

-Matthew 19: 26

Is It Possible
by

Hazel F. Adams

Is it possible? It is only possible when you have the courage to make it so. It's only possible when in your heart you believe it to be. It's only possible when you have the faith, and trust that you can change reality.

So change the world, dream the impossible dream and make it come true. Is it possible to overcome the roadblocks, setbacks, and valleys in life? Yes it's possible but it's not based on what you say, but what you believe in and do.

Is it possible to make a positive difference in the world? Yes if you search deep within yourself, build a level of self-confidence and believe in a higher power. There are no limits or boundaries; you can reach for the stars, the moon, or even an ivory tower. Yes, it is possible.

" We give thanks to God always for you all, making mention of you in our prayers; remembering without ceasing your work of faith, and labor of love, and patience of hope in our Lord Jesus Christ, in the sight of our Father God."

-I Thessalonians 1:2-3

To the Pastor
by

Hazel F. Adams

As we celebrate your first anniversary as Pastor
of this Church, we wish to express our appreciation,
for we thank you very much.

We thank you for your fine leadership and for the
sermons that you preach, you are truly a Bible
scholar, this is shown by the methods you use to
teach.

Your time and your effort have been very well spent
as you share with us the Bible study Scriptures from
the old and new testaments.

Your sharing and caring spirit has helped the church
and the community, and today we say thank you for
your spirit of Humanity.

So continue on in the name of Jesus, and let His
praise resound. And by His grace and mercy lead
us on to higher ground

Love and best wishes to you and your family on this
special day. And may God forever bless you in his
own special way.

" Finally, brethren, farewell. Be perfect, be of good comfort, be of one mind, live in peace; and the God of love and peace shall be with you."

-II Corinthians 13:11

Moving On
To My Dear Friends
by
Hazel F. Adams

As you move to a new location let Jesus be your guide, and keep those loving Christian spirits for God will stay by your side.

You are really wonderful people and we knew that from the start. The Christian love you shared with us will remain when we are apart.

It was just a beautiful blessing that God sent you two our way, and the song ministry you leave with us in our hearts will forever stay.

You will be missed here at Mount Olive, please keep in touch, and just know that our church family loves you and will miss you very much.

We will miss you. Take the Lord with you.

"In that day, saith the Lord of hosts, shall ye call every man his neighbor under the vine and under the fig tree."

-Zechariah 3:10

To My Neighbor
by
Hazel Adams

We will miss you for we love you. Please don't fail to keep in touch.

Your good neighbor gesture has meant so very much.

You are just a kind, caring person who has inspired me day by day. There is just something special about you. And I thank God for people like you, whenever I kneel to pray.

I pray that God will richly bless you as you move to another home. For you will be a blessing to others no matter where you roam.

We ponder and we wonder, why things change day by day. We truly know that whatever happens God will surly make the way.

But he, willing to justify himself, said unto Jesus, "and who is my neighbor?"

"Trust in the Lord with all thine heart; and lean not unto thine own understanding. In all thy ways acknowledge him, and he shall direct thy paths."

Proverbs 3: 5-6

Confused
by

Dell R. Adams

Is it real or is it fake
Is it give or take
Is it a dream?
Am I asleep or awake?
Who knows, who cares?
Is it a lie or the truth
What brought you here?
What got you there?
Does it really matter?
Can you touch it?
Can you feel it?
What's the need? Will you follow
Or will you lead?
Don't know, where will you go
What's the limit?
Can you reach it, can you last?
Do you know, do you care?
Confused?

"For which cause we faint not; but though our outward man perish, yet the inward man is renewed day by day."

-II Corinthians 4: 16

Get Well
by

Hazel F. Adams

The best blessings come in the stillness of the day. In the peace of the quiet haven we can let Jesus have his way.

He is always there, He can always hear our prayer. God has that healing touch. The strength and healing touch.

Blessed be his holy name. He heals and takes care.

May God ever grant you perfect health and restore healing to you.

Often times we wonder just what to do and say, in times of distress and trials or when illness comes our way. There is a God who cares about you each and every day.

He knows just how much we can bear, for when the load gets too heavy for us, He is willing our load to share.

For when I awake in the morning and start on the day, I thank God for His goodness and for the blessings He sends my way.

" And we know that all things work together for good to them who love God, to them who are the called according to His purpose."

- Romans 8:28